YOUR KNOWLEDGE HAS VALUE

- We will publish your bachelor's and master's thesis, essays and papers

- Your own eBook and book - sold worldwide in all relevant shops

- Earn money with each sale

Upload your text at www.GRIN.com
and publish for free

Bibliographic information published by the German National Library:

The German National Library lists this publication in the National Bibliography; detailed bibliographic data are available on the Internet at http://dnb.dnb.de .

This book is copyright material and must not be copied, reproduced, transferred, distributed, leased, licensed or publicly performed or used in any way except as specifically permitted in writing by the publishers, as allowed under the terms and conditions under which it was purchased or as strictly permitted by applicable copyright law. Any unauthorized distribution or use of this text may be a direct infringement of the author s and publisher s rights and those responsible may be liable in law accordingly.

Imprint:

Copyright © 2013 GRIN Verlag
Print and binding: Books on Demand GmbH, Norderstedt Germany
ISBN: 9783668139824

This book at GRIN:

https://www.grin.com/document/314354

Nico Grünewälder

The Impact of Crude Oil in Nigeria. A Blessing or a Curse?

GRIN Verlag

GRIN - Your knowledge has value

Since its foundation in 1998, GRIN has specialized in publishing academic texts by students, college teachers and other academics as e-book and printed book. The website www.grin.com is an ideal platform for presenting term papers, final papers, scientific essays, dissertations and specialist books.

Visit us on the internet:

http://www.grin.com/

http://www.facebook.com/grincom

http://www.twitter.com/grin_com

THE IMPACT OF CRUDE OIL IN NIGERIA

Written by:

Nico Gruenewaelder

Faculty of Management

Vancouver Island University

Nanaimo, BC, Canada

November 26th, 2013

Table of Contents

ABSTRACT 1

INTRODUCTION 1

LITERATURE REVIEW 2

DATA ANALYSIS 3

CONCLUSION 3

APPENDIX 5

REFERENCES 7

Abstract

This paper examines the question as to whether crude oil resource is a blessing or curse to Nigeria. Since the discovery of crude oil in Nigeria the economy of Nigeria has improved, increasing the GDP through the sales of oil barrels abroad. The paper observes that the blessings from crude oil resource in Nigeria at large takes the form of increased government revenues, increased export earnings, the attendant improvement, opportunities and linkage effects in the economy. However the paper is majorly going to focus on the variables between the increased GDP and the increase poverty level. This paper is of the view that crude oil resource is more of curse than a blessing to the Nigerian economy.

Introduction

The origin of oil exploration and exploitation started in 1859, where the first oil well was drilled by Edwin L. Darke. This was the first time crude oil was discovered in commercial quantity at Oloibiri in the present day Bayelsa State in Nigeria (Tamuno, 2006). However, serious and sustained efforts did not happen until Shell Darcy Petroleum Company commenced operation in 1956. As the local demand for these products increased, two major oil companies - Shell and British Petroleum - formed a 50/50 joint venture refining company in Nigeria: The Nigerian Petroleum Refining Company (NPRC) in 1960. The NPRC built a 38,000b/d refinery at Alesa-Eleme near Port-Harcourt to refine local crude (Tamuno, 2006). The impact of crude oil in the Nigerian economy has a paradoxical effect in the sense that it should have only positive impact on the economy and the population, but this is not the case. Wealth generated by oil revenues has not passed down to the citizens of Nigeria: around 70% of the population still lives below the poverty line. For many years Nigeria's oil industry has been plagued by corruption and mismanagement. The United Nations has estimated that as a result of corruption, 80% of energy revenues in the country only benefit 1% of the population (United Nations, 2003). This topic was chosen specifically to analyze the changes the economy has had from the time the crude oil was found till now and why the economy is not growing and developing as it should. From the graphs below one can see the increase in the GDP of the economy and would expect that the poverty level should decrease as a result but that is not the case because as the GDP increases so does the poverty level. This paper is going to analyze effect of crude oil on the Nigerian economy. We examine the correlation between fuel exports and GDP per capita growth, and poverty headcount ratio between 1960 and 2012. The central-question is: How did crude oil affect the economic growth and the poverty of Nigeria?

Literature Review

In his paper "Nigeria's oils sector and the poor", Michael L. Ross points out that oil plays a key role in Nigerian economic and politics. Nigeria has a high dependency on oil and thus suffers from multiple problems which are known to affect oil dependent countries. The five major problems described in his paper are an instable economy, suppression of other economic sectors, rise in inequality, risk of civil war, and increasing corruption (Ross, 2003). Nearly the same conclusion is drawn in Dr. Mark Rhodes paper "The Importance of Oil to an Export Dependent Economy: The Case of Nigeria". For a country depending highly on natural resources, a rise in prices of these resources like oil leads to an increased GDP and a growth in GDP therefore does not always implicate an economic growth (Rhodes and Suleiman, 2013).

Data Analysis

The data we are using is provided by the World Bank from 2012. This data includes about 1300 socio-economic indicators from which we are using only fuel exports growth, GDP per capita growth, and poverty headcount ratio between 1960 and 2012. The data for the poverty headcount ratio are only provided for certain years (Table 2). We conduct a linear regression analysis to identify a correlation between fuel exports growth and GDP per capita growth. To perform this analysis we are using the statistic-software Stata 12. The slope parameter of 0.133159 illustrates a moderate uphill relationship between fuel exports growth and GDP per capita growth of Nigeria (Table 3). An increasing fuel exports growth of one percent leads to an increase in GDP per capita growth of about 0.13 percent. The p-value of 0.002 shows a statistically significant result (Table 3). The GDP per capita increased from $92.81 in 1960 to $1,555.41 in 2012, which shows an annual average growth of 5.46% (Table 1). The poverty headcount ratio has increased from 53.93% in 1986 to 67.98% in 2010 (Table 2). Despite the intense growth of the GDP per capita which is commonly associated with a decrease in poverty, the example of Nigeria shows the opposite (Roemer and Gugerty, 1997).

Conclusion

From the above data carried out we can see that as the GDP per capita increased from $92.81 in 1960 to $1,555.41 in 2012, so did the poverty ratio increase from 53.93% in 1986 to 67.98% in 2010. This goes to show that the increase in GDP does not reduce the poverty level. For this challenge, we suggest that the Federal Government of Nigeria should put in place appropriate measures to stem further mismanagement of revenue derived from export of crude oil and make realistic monetary and fiscal policies that will help alleviate the suffering of the Nigerian people. Provide a 'beacon of hope' for reform, and may catalyze further changes in the oil sector. Developing the Natural gas sector, Nigeria has vast natural gas reserves, which will soon be a major source of income. Natural gas is generally sold through long-term contracts, which tend to reduce the volatility of revenues; natural gas is also more environmentally-friendly than oil. Upgrading the government's decaying oil refineries, by contracting out their management to private firms. A better refining capacity will both ease domestic gas shortages, and open the door towards more value-added industries. When the government is highly dependent on oil revenues, it will be plagued with corruption and rent-seeking; it will also be harder to consolidate democratic reforms; again the poor will suffer (Energy Information Agency, 2003). These problems may be best resolved through reforms of the non-oil sector. One strategy would be for Nigeria to adopt the Indonesian approach: diversify the economy by promoting manufacturing and agriculture through public investments and market-friendly reforms. As the non-oil sector grows, the dependence of the government and economy on the oil sector will diminish.

Appendix

Table 1

Table 2

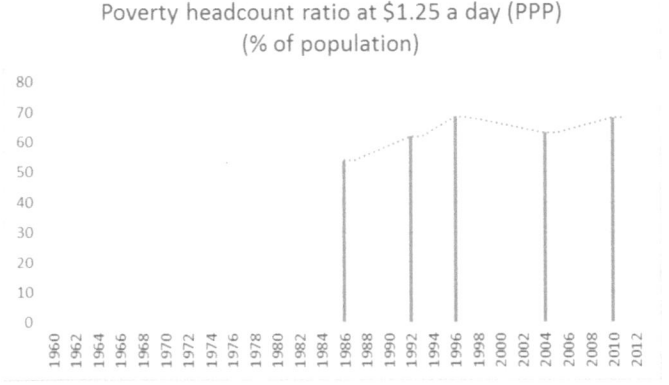

Table 3

```
. reg GDPp fuel
```

Source	SS	df	MS			
Model	520.246976	1	520.246976	Number of obs	=	33
Residual	1353.45309	31	43.6597771	$F(1, 31)$	=	11.92
				Prob > F	=	0.0016
				R-squared	=	0.2777
				Adj R-squared	=	0.2544
				Root MSE	=	6.6076
Total	1873.70007	32	58.5531271			

GDPpercapitagr~h	Coef.	Std. Err.	t	P>|t|	[95% Conf. Interval]	
fuelexportgrowth	.133159	.0385751	3.45	0.002	.0544847	.2118333
_cons	.9011271	1.210051	0.74	0.462	-1.566788	3.369042

References

Rhodes, M. and Suleiman, T. 2013. The Importance of Oil to an Export Dependent Economy: The Case of Nigeria. Available at SSRN 2307636.

Roemer, M. & Gugerty, M. K. 1997. Does economic growth reduce poverty? CAER II.

Ross, M. 2003. Nigeria's oil sector and the poor. Position Paper for DFID-Nigeria, UCLA, Los Angeles.

TheWorldBank. 2013. Nigeria | Data. [online] Available at: http://data.worldbank.org/country/nigeria [Accessed: 24 Nov 2013].

Energy Information Agency. 2013. U.S. Energy Information Administration (EIA). [online] Available at: http://eia.doe.gov/emeu/cabs/nigeria.html [Accessed: 24 Nov 2013].

Osaghae, E. 1994. "The Ogoni Uprising: Oil Politics, Minority Agitation, and the Future of the Nigerian State" African Affairs 94, pp 325-344.

Tamuno, S. 2006 African journal online: Crude oil recourses a blessing or a curse to Nigeria volume 4. pp53-58.

United Nations Development Program. 2003. "Human Development Report" [Online]. Available: http://hdr.undp.org/reports/global.

World Bank. 2002. World Development Report 2000/2001: Attacking Poverty. New York: World Bank and Oxford University Press.

YOUR KNOWLEDGE HAS VALUE

- We will publish your bachelor's and master's thesis, essays and papers

- Your own eBook and book - sold worldwide in all relevant shops

- Earn money with each sale

Upload your text at www.GRIN.com
and publish for free